ACRES OF LIGHT

Acres *of* Light

KATHERINE GALLAGHER

2016

Published by Arc Publications
Nanholme Mill, Shaw Wood Road,
Todmorden OL14 6DA, UK
www.arcpublications.co.uk

Copyright © Katherine Gallagher, 2016
Copyright in the present edition © Arc Publications, 2016
Design by Tony Ward
Printed by Lightning Source

978 1910345 73 3 (pbk)
978 1910345 74 0 (hbk)
978 1910345 75 7 (ebk)

The cover painting is by Pierre Vella,
by kind permission of the artist.

Editor for the UK and Ireland:
John W. Clarke

for Bernard and Julien

CONTENTS

MOTHER TONGUE

I have changed
from myself into myself
from moment to moment

sprung into fragments
on the word path

Mother tongue
you piece me together

a human mosaic

ROSE AUSLÄNDER
(tr. Jean Boase-Beier)

I
Green Groves and Flowering Almond

ELAN

(Holland Park)

Under leafing chestnuts, flowering almond,
cherry, April gathers a blanket-greening,
tendrils float.

A boy plays *Summertime* on a sax,
practises over and over. Now he tries
Scarborough Fair – silky,

lissom. I walk lightheaded, heels
gliding, in love with all this –
the halcyon afternoon, its warming breeze...

A peacock, tail-fanned, struts, dazzles
among daisies, daffodils. Children's voices
split the air. Islands of chat echo,

grass grows beneath us: minute blades stir,
flicker – something is happening – a season
emptying into the moment, rinsing clean.

A MEASURE OF STILLNESS

Through yellowed wheat, sunflowers,
along straight roads sparse with trees,
summer's haze shearing the air,
suddenly rising above the plain,
the non-identical spires.

As I drive closer,
the cathedral seems to disappear
among tower-blocks,
factories, streets zigzagging
around mediaeval hills –

this pilgrimage to Chartres
where I am learning
to take my cue
from its heart –
its dance in space –

to never take my eyes
from the spires, the bowl,
the ark lifting
burning
into a teal sky.

THE SPELL OF FIREFLIES

I like mirrors, miracles and handouts,
being in love, telling people I care
and sometimes talking to myself. I tend to think there's
mostly a way out, and that one can count on surprises
such as unicorns and fireflies.

At a pinch, I believe in time-pieces, hair extensions and fake tans,
a sugar-free diet, and testing chairs for comfort.
Love can make you wise to the future,
laced with a just-right, wake-up tale. I believe in
sprinting the extra mile and in happy days for optimists.

I like to think there's good in vitamin-pills
and know you can't make a garden in a rush.
I prefer a minimum of walls and a roof with
windows. Sometimes I am stunned
by the comeback of the moment.

Icebergs, oceans and Arctic skies are in the same count
as polar bears. I shall continue to rely on the bedrock of rice
and raspberries, while still trying to place
the bigger picture – winners and losers
on their dizzying slopes.

GHAZAL: THE FIRE

When your heart grips and won't let go, it's fire;
don't fear it. Hear it, say it could be fire.

Though your dream has not been easy, you think it's true;
grab the chance, this dance. Embrace the fire.

When you hear the words that chase and race your days
along new shores, believe. It must be fire.

Don't hesitate and bait the silence, there's no recipe
for those who wait for love: trust the fire.

When a voice inside you flicks the switch
and a million sparks ignite, you think it's fire.

When you wake on the breaking edge of wanting more,
and read the fine-print as before, you're sure it's fire.

When you catch the dream up-close, it lives in you,
keeps you in its glow. You know it's fire.

CREDO

I believe in witches, flying fish, stars,
the stern existence of moons,
Elizabeth Bishop's wanderlust, Plath's
metaphors, the blessing of macaroons.

I believe in dancers, high-tech and chance,
that bonhomie of the Goons,
the wily stuff of breakthroughs,
and turtles claiming the dunes.

I believe in walking the talk,
a diet with plenty of prunes,
in Baudelaire's not eating his words,
and the Beatles' flyaway tunes.

I believe in the terror of Teflon,
in about-turns and desperate high noons,
the slow fire of Jabba the Hutt,
and occasional savage new brooms.

TURNABOUT

My room is no longer itself,
the carpet an old painting worn
threadbare with being looked at.

The windows chafe and rattle –
unsettled as children
waiting for a party.

My computer glares back at me,
an accusing spectator
wanting the action to start.

Mirror, that tease,
has its busybody eye
on everything.

My rows of books sit
disconsolate,
desperate for air –

all this restlessness, the plot
on hold. And the door so aware
it holds itself ajar.

PORT DES BARQUES, LATE AUGUST

The postcard reaches end to end:
a perfect wraparound –
fishing-huts to the left, alongside sunbathers,
paddling children, swimmers loving their patch of sand.

I'm tempted to jump in, the waves insistent –
that bluest-of-blue draw of the sea,
a voice telling me to dive, take a chance
before the wind lifts, frisks the air,
before the postcard cools.

QUOTIDIAN

(after a line by Mahmoud Darwish,
'We love life whenever we can.')

We love life whenever we can.
We like to hear the robin getting started.
We stop and listen, entranced by how
we love life, and the life of the robin.

We love when children gallop to school
clutching their frisbees, satchels, racing the day.
In them, we see again ourselves, aspiring, happy.
We love life whenever we can.

We love life when we taste spring air
and walk under the prunus, singing haiku in our street
while bees buzz in the gardens, with no time to lose,
and sun warms the butterflies' first flights.

We love the open bay, its gulls insistent
and if we're lucky, we hear dolphins whistle
to each other. This is time we have underlined,
remembering what we've done, where we're going.

We love our dreams and our journeys, long past,
those yet to be taken. We love this buoyancy
carrying us from one season to the next.
We love life whenever we can.

II
LOVE-SONGS FROM AFAR

I COULD HAVE BEEN BORN IN A TAXI

speeding in at the last minute
through Maldon's volcanic hills,
chasing history and voices –
so much gone, like the gold;
and, a mini-volcano-in-waiting: me,
setting the pace as it were –
my mother concentrating,
contractions every few minutes…

I wasn't ready yet to be born;
too soon for she and I
to meet face to face, hold
a real conversation,
me with my strange eye
on everything,
about to learn the beauty out there
to be settled in the eye of the beholder.

ODYSSEY

*'The danger of travelling
is how it takes you over'*

Remembering the lights of a hundred cities
and not quite belonging –
arriving by motorway, train or plane,
sucked into streets of languages
controlling locales, time, the air.

Which way, a thrum of questions, adapting lines
pidgin speak, as each city revealed
its minarets and spires, the glasshouses
of a chameleon century...
                              Europe
rocking backwards and forwards on rundown heels,
still mourning its dead: London, stitched into her brain
from childhood, an Australian-British schooling
when the Empire stretched a scarlet blanket
across the globe – Victoriana, Dickens,
wrought iron on pillared backdrops,
the veined streets of a city's heart,
its folklored history, an inheritance.

RINGS

(i.m. my mother)

Living a hemisphere away,
I couldn't have her cherry-wood
bookshelf, her piano or T.V.,
she left me her engagement ring –
four small diamonds on a bridge,

and a dress-ring I'd always admired –
a ruby set inside a hoof-shaped curl of gold,
a *Ponte Vecchio* souvenir from her trip to Florence,
a nod to the gambler in me. She'd smile
to know I wear it every day, believe it brings me luck –
a talisman that brailled me through fog
as I drove out of Brecon in Wales,

the same gold charm I lost
and found again on Bexhill beach.

Make your own luck, it tells me, as she
wedded to her days, made hers.

MY MOTHER'S HORSE-SHOE RING

(after Grace Nichols)

Sometimes when I see it
on my index finger
I am reassured,

rub its ruby stone, her gift.
I need this small reminder
of her, its lucky charm

that catches me
like an itinerant fire
chipped from the sun.

Each year she went on safari,
a holiday away – time to take stock,
rest. She loved Daylesford
with its tree-spaces: once a mining town,
now a spa, surrounded by wattle-gums
and pines, with a sea-blue lake:
a furore of gardens, delectable, idyllic.

She'd meander about old haunts, writing
in a pavement café or visiting a gallery.
Was a week away enough? She'd laugh,
say she'd missed us – her schoolgirl daughters
managing the household, practising
her know-how. *She was proud of us…*
It was what we wanted to hear,
we believed her.

LONESOME TONIGHT

Standing with his push-bike friends
he'd watch me pass along the street
crazy about me – a way of saying
I should enjoy it, forget gravitas.

Finally sheer fervour won.
I drifted off to films with him,
waited for a spark. Kindness couldn't cut it
as he kissed me cold and hot...

I watched him throw old dancing partners
shoulder-high and wished for someone
interested in books. *Why me?*
I couldn't jitterbug to save my life.

THE MASTERY OF HORSES

I hate to admit I'm afraid of horses –
those long angular heads and cavernous mouths.
So much face, big-lidded eyes on the corners,
ears flicking forward, back. And the horse-brain
in there – cagey, non-standard, quick.

Take brumbies – the way they grip
a mountain at speed, wild beasts galloping wide,
masters of terrain as they race full pelt.
Impossible to imagine them as farm horses,
tamed, cut off from their feral lives.

I watched my father train a yearling,
our latest farm hack – cajoling, threatening,
sometimes lashing with a leather whip –
the young horse whinnying, rising on its hind legs,
tugging against the halter, mouth frothing.
'You have to let them know who's boss,' he said.

Years later, out riding. My filly bolts…
Desperate, hanging on to her mane
for surely the countdown, I hear my father's words
zigzag around me, see only sky – the traffic of air.

FARM DAM, EASTVILLE

(i.m. Joe)

There was swimming –
a paradise of dog-paddle and dive –
the dam's mudded elegance with its khaki yellows
inviting bars of sun to interrupt shade
from a ring of eucalypts. It draws us in,
we're your pupils, siblings
learning the friendliness of water.

'Swim to me', I hear you say:
slowly we feel our lightness in this
measure of waves. And beyond the momentum
of those days, there is a silence of remembering:
blankets of water slide over our heads.

FINDING THE PRINCE

To reach him she would have to go back
to her old haunts, suburbs she had left.

Would he announce himself with a glass slipper?
That was the catch. The parents

would have to organise a dance
as they'd done in the old days.

There would be waltzes, murmurings of touch.
It might be love at first sight

though this was not a necessity.
Godmothers would be there

to splash them with advice.
Their palace would be simple – a bungalow,

squat at the end of a long road
with houses all looking much the same

and a kitchen ready for laughter and children,
matching chairs, a table set just like an advert.

She would smile at her prince. They would kiss
ready to be happy ever after.

III
STORMS AND THE BREATH OF OWLS

RIVERBOAT

Leisurely through Shepperton to Hampton Court,
following the Thames, late April: boatmen stop, lift the sluices.

Travellers are enveloped by cherry blossoms,
birdsong, swans. Couples mark this journey –

love makes them luminous, heroic,
as sun shimmies along the water,

pierces their lightweight shirts.
Do they trust the weather – clouds and rain hanging

overhead? They are counting on chances,
gathering depths in the mystery of elements,

their biggest gamble of the day,
whirlpools, undertow –

the margins they've yet to reach,
voyaging them on beyond themselves.

BEFORE THE STORM

(after Bergh's *Nordic Summer Evening*)

The northern sky filters light
                                over the lake
She, satin-resplendent, stiff-backed,
                                        is dressed for dinner. He too
city-smart in suit and tie. Neither of them
                                        looks at the other.

What keeps them so enclosed within themselves?

Arms clasped behind her, she's braced for
                                any outcomes.

Casually, he gazes over the lake.

                        Such distance between them,
are they homed by silences?

They have all the time
                        of figures on a frieze.

BIRTHDAY OWL

(for Julien)

When you brought it to me
wrapped in blue paper, tied with tinselly ribbon,

I opened it gingerly, surprised at your miniature gift:
faceted crystal, one inch tall,

set on a tiny plinth – unblinking topaz eyes
a shining creature, conduit for light.

You picked it up, *t'-whit-t'-whoo*-ed,
gliding around the room, the night forest close

with eerie calls, a witch's moon, and you
a six-year-old in love with this

glass-feathered bird
on its unbreakable perch –

our barn owl swooping –
in, out – in and out,

daring the sky…

CHOICES

I go to the hedge of our holiday-cottage
to trim branches within easy reach.
I am cutting edgily until two eyes
fix mine. Not a sound passes between us,
but we understand each other.
The blackbird on her nest is intent.
Without a second look, I withdraw,
murmuring apologies.

PALMERSTON ROAD, SUNDAY MID-MORNING, N22

A shameless blue
totally without shadow.

A squirrel scurries into the ivy,
sparrows swoop on the feeder
and forsythia hikes its yellow skyward.
Not a single car edges through
this birdsong-echoing street.

For once they've lined up
on the side of nature
and stayed immobile – for that pause
when earth listens to itself.

Owl stared hard: it gave no answers.
Mummy had been gone for days.
I faced Owl; it only stared
and blinked. Nanny said that we'd see
Mummy soon. I told Sissy
she was coming back. I feared that
Owl might fly away –
but it only blinked and blinked.

Nanny said to draw Owl
if we liked. She got us down white paper
and some pens. Sissy cried for she was
only three. She drew Owl
in criss-cross lines of red. I made Owl
deep brown with a ring around each eye.

The fierce winds shrieked and crashed against the glass
rattling panes so we could hardly hear.
I wanted quiet Owl to stay. Nanny said
we'd give the pictures to our Mum.
I told Sissy she would be back soon.
When I looked again, our Owl had flown.

A CAUTIONARY TALE

Mildred loves babies but was thirty-eight
before she got the feeling –
I've left it rather late,
all my freewheeling.

Here she was, Mildred,
our old seventies' flat-share
who'd said she'd rather be dead
than have babies in her hair.

Now she couldn't afford to wait:
pure misery, *to be or not to be* –
it's all suddenly down to fate,
and serendipity.

And her with this terrible urge –
what had happened to romance:
IVF, post-coital tests, a surge
of last-minute angst, last chance?

RAILWAY FIELDS TANKA

(for D. B.)

Monet
at Railway Fields –
what does he make of it
stalking trees
that have grown with him?

A baby robin
in the Japanese knotweed
chirps all afternoon –
one call after another,
urgent, urgent.

Sun sliding down
behind the houses:
sky salmon pink
minute on minute,
slinking into black.

BEATLES POEM

Let it Be, Strawberry Fields, Yellow Submarine,
my students who'd never known Elvis suddenly fired up –
the Fab Four going from *Love Me Do* and *A Hard Day's Night*
to songs to hang your heart on: *Michelle, Yesterday,*
Nowhere Man, Eleanor Rigby... and... Just when
you thought you'd heard it all, *Imagine*
and *Hey, Jude.*

John, Paul, Ringo and *George* – they couldn't replace Elvis
the way no one can replace your teen years – but soon
all over the planet, no one was too young or too old
anymore. No one would walk on air quite the same way again.
Even when the Beatles broke up, their songs held them together.
Even when John Lennon was shot, and we mourned him,
no one could shoot down the songs.

HAIKU

clearing sky –
the impossible nearness
of stars

cherry blossoms –
the clip-clop of horses
distant now

evening stillness –
on the hillside
the stillness of sheep

autumn morning –
a rain-soaked rose
sways in the breeze

inside the robin's
pure song –
evening walk

winter solstice –
the darkness closes in
against the church bells

chilly mouthfuls of air
wintering
my tongue

Note: The haiku is a Japanese poetic form made up of three lines with a total of 17 syllables arranged 5-7-5. Many haiku poets simply follow that pattern. However, English-language poets world-wide increasingly dispense with the 17-syllable count. 'The spirit of haiku often identifies it more than the meter. The essential elements are brevity, immediacy, spontaneity and sudden illumination. That flash of awareness is crucial'. (John Drury. The Poetry Dictionary, 1950) The actual discarding of the conventional pattern 5-7-5 is largely due to a lack of equivalences between English and Japanese – 17 syllables in Japanese does not necessarily equate to 17 syllables in English.

IV
CONSTELLATIONS AND A SPACE OF OCEANS

THE DREAM IS THE OCEAN

The ocean calls the dolphin
      The dolphin calls the wave
The wave calls the sun
      The sun calls the coral
The coral calls the colour
      The colour calls the fire
The fire calls the moment
      The moment calls the light
The light calls the shine
      The shine calls the spray
The spray calls the deep
      The deep calls the dolphin
The dolphin calls the dream
      The dream is the ocean

LEMON GUMS

(corymbia citriodora)

Sometimes you come across lines
of them bordering a road –
dove-grey, satin-barked eucalypts:
trunks that no one has written on,
carved their name or the date.

Indeed, miraculous that no one
felt the need to blemish such skin,
but allowed it to crinkle with years,
ageing at its own pace, the svelte branches
reaching into shades of sky.

On both sides of the road, these sentinels,
in perfumed silence over long summers,
settle into being admired as works of art:
even graffitists stand back,
pocket their knives.

BEES

A pollen-laden bee is weaving about,
circling the flowers as a spider waits, traps it
in its web.

Desperate, the intrepid prisoner
re-invents itself as warrior; wings dipping,
legs lashing the silky bars.
Slowly the web changes to a golden net
as the bee unloads its pollen.

Unable to interfere, I tear myself away,
returning an hour later
to find a circle of golden spokes –

the bee, nowhere to be seen.

THE MOUNTAIN

On sunny days, the mountain turns quite blue,
takes on the azure sparkle of the sky –
always a place to dream of coming to,

to feel that snowy-crunch beneath your shoe,
or soar across a piste that's powder-dry.
On sunny days, the mountain turns quite blue –

you feel the silence is in love with you,
invites a quietude no one can buy
in this wild place you dream of coming to.

The snow melts earlier now, the view
quite changed, and not so lovely to the eye;
on sunny days, the mountain turns quite blue.

It's clear that tales of acid rain are true
as ragged trees suggest they'll surely die
in this wild place you dream of coming to.

Its hazy beauty strangely keeps it new,
helps you forget the damage or the why.
On sunny days, the mountain turns quite blue –
this lumened place you dream of coming to.

SNOW

sashays
finds its own
borders

is prodigal
like someone
with loose money
showering gifts
on passing landscapes

a white meld,
the gigantic tableau
of its giving
steady

a flaring weald
of mesmerising
silences –
occasional birds dipping
in a muslin sky

snow's gypsy heart
tinkering
and snow-dreamers
at their windows
watching

as it dusts the hills,
valleys, or thickens
in squalls

THE BRIEF OF TRAVELLING

I pitch my tent
on the edge of the desert,

watch the helter-skelter mirages:
savour the journey's spell.

My trek is restless for found treasure –
flaring birdsong, for rivers that unfold.

It has blind trails like a bushwalker's maze,
the weather white-wearing hot.

It has its terrors of forgetting,
stark monuments and forbidden marsh.

It has its long-sighted crafty Crusoe,
its footloose wily Gulliver.

ODE TO THE BOEING 747

Winged lurcher
without the heart of a bird,

shining voyager
that rides all clouds,

nets turbulence
within a breakaway field;

that engines homewards
through the grace of air –

you are discoverer of day
turning night,

sun streaking
the globe's jagged edges,

unwrapping temperatures
in the grip of each now.

When you leave in the night,
you arrow through darkness

magicking this turnabout of skies
to mark the stars

differently – your steady jumbo-
delivery across hemispheres,

homaging the journey –
ways forward and back.

COMING INTO ZURICH

A wing-tip draws its arc
over the valley, a city clasping
a river to itself. This plane-travel
is the riskiest thing I do,
following clouds as though
my life depends upon it,
skeining in my nerves
as we dip over
yellowed hills, ploughed fields...

Again we tilt, hills lifting
in, out – the plane carrying us,
its lean shadow stretching ahead –

suddenly in the cabin
a hush of togetherness,
its rope tightening, binding us close,
closer in gravity's pull
as we will ourselves down,
the plane steady, holding.

TERROR

I can be miniscule,
fool you with echoes.

Whole cities tremble
in my wake.

Danger holds me
bone-close.

I use it well, taunt days
with omens.

Rewards don't
beguile me.

I am part of folklore,
lines drawn in dust.

BULLIES

With the eye in the back of his head
he sees them coming –

eight-year-old breakers,
baby-hard, baby-soft.

Their elegant space-machine
could swallow him,

drown him once and for all
in a dish of air.

He freezes
as they expect

though a voice inside him squeaks *I...*
Words cut his tongue,

weigh in his mind
like a bruise.

MOUSE IN A TRAP

(after George Grosz)

The trap has closed on its neck –
body bloated, tail straight,
fur and whiskers bristling.

Its hind legs hang,
two sticks with nowhere to go.
The eyes are wide, glassed-in terror –
a small animal still in its own skin.

You glance back at the spindly shanks
that gave way, the dangling
forepaws that lost their grip.

PHOTOGRAPH – MEKONG DELTA, SOUTH VIETNAM, 1965

The woman's hands
are tied behind her back –

her hands are not allowed
to speak for her.

The interrogator lays his knife
across her throat.

Another woman close by,
hands folded,

understands the price
of being still.

REFUGEES AT THE AID CENTRE, DEGHABUR, ETHIOPIA

The tapered fingers of her gaunt hands,
a version of her child's...
She caresses him, his fists opening,
closing, drawing down the sun.

Her eyes beg, the face of one more parent
in the queue. She smiles into her hands,
arms enfolding the child as if
her carrying will never be over.
She will keep holding him, offering
water, milk, a spoonful of rice...

The child, innocent of the fight around him,
wages his own battle, whimpers,
sinks into his mother. Another day.

IRELAND, 1972

I

Nationalism's postures
hunt like shadows

Ireland's shadows
worn to a blur

Stars have no shadows
in the now

We are fashioned
sleep-wise

and the deep anguish
of belonging
is a starved knot

II

Artistic hells are free to
let nothing drop

to make sure that no shred
that should be held
escapes

Here amongst civil war
they quote Yeats

Some say he was a fascist
want to leave it there

For others
he is still doing
his homework

III

Meanwhile
holiday-people
grip the edge
of the sea

farmers sheath
another harvest
and the Connemara waterfall
keeps negotiating
the slow-fast spin of things

water's grey face
on bedraggled stone

bedraggled as
Ireland's history

glimpses of tangents
the hunt in the air for
rainbow crystals
real gems

V
ACRES OF LIGHT
(i.m. Kevin)

GOING BACK TO THE FARM

Call it *'Home'* as it catches you on the road through Shelbourne –
a shape in the distance, the house you both built.

You move along the Three Chain Road, a time of breaking the
    mould –
after operations, dark hopes, intensive care –

nearly not making it back. Finally, patched up, you
came home, to spend last days in the shades of all you knew:

the whirl of the shearing shed,
the plough and harvester...

SERENITY PRAYER

(after A.A.)

Let it enter your heart,

be the hope of your being.

Everywhere you turn,

light follows, takes you

across borders

that dissolve into

the measure of your days.

THE TELLING

I knew your condition
was worsening, couldn't believe
your body's intermittent jerks,
fever, your skin's revolt –
farmer-brother, still young;
planter of twenty-thousand wattles,
she-oaks, banksias,
ironbarks.

Be brave, believe.
The omens aren't good, you said.

YOUR STORY

The weather-forecast has taken over your time –
what you would give to trees, on their behalf,
your ultimatums to the sky.
Around you, the scratched paddocks gleam palely.

The blue hills are a singing range of fur,
the tremendous ache of mirage
spreading itself almost neatly
deliciously, ahead; its sheen
that keeps you looking.

For thirty years, you listened to the news and gossip
of the *Country Hour,*
farming snippets – *dos and don'ts* –
the present settling futures.

EASTVILLE SONATA

Rain, long-awaited, thrusts
against the window –
finally, a breakthrough.

Under our toes is mud. The ground is soggy
with the rain's waltzing.
The sky is into frolics
steadying against rafters of cloud.

We hear new notes,
their shine shot through with sun –
washing us with the beauty of rain.

RETROSPECT

You lived your life in the shambles of weather,
studied it, knew its provenance,
and over time, accepted, learned
to shield your day with it.

You called in the black swans
and the water around them,
built the dams, the welcoming oases.
They are in our veins
we taste them in the air,
learning survival's truths,
its patterns of water.

Golden wattle   across
the Whipstick   loneliness
thermoses of tea   sugaring it
stirring with a stick   sticks on the ground
travelling back   bone-secrets
and back   yours now

THE SHEARING-SHED

In the shed at Eastville, the sheep lost their coats,
took on a lighter skin.

Today I see you at the wool-table
throwing the fleeces, their edges smooth
under your hands.

There is a rhythm of waiting.
                    The sheep don't hesitate,
skid down the race to freedom.
                    You count them proudly
in and out
                    towards another year.

THE PRESENCE OF THE TREES

The cemetery sand is newly piled over,
and around is a trail of birds, eucalypts,
native plants – boronia, heath.

Your drug was the love of breakaway,
a fine cutting free. Under the fiercest sun,
you have worn the beauty of flowers:

gum-blossom, mimosa, banksias, that the sun bakes
through acres of light.
I imagine you here, being yourself, striding

beneath a theatre of stars.

KATHERINE GALLAGHER was born in Maldon, Victoria, in 1935, graduated from the University of Melbourne in 1963 and taught in Melbourne for five years before moving to Europe, living first in London and then in Paris for nine years. In 1979 she moved back to London, working as a secondary teacher and after 1990, as a poetry tutor for the Open College of the Arts, Jackson's Lane, Barnet College and Torriano, London. During this time she co-edited *Poetry London* as well as working extensively with primary school children. She has poems in over forty-five children's anthologies.

In 1978, she was awarded a New Writer's Fellowship from the Literature Board, Australia Council, and in 1981, she won the Brisbane Warana Poetry Prize. Her book *Passengers to the City* (Hale & Iremonger, Sydney, 1985) was shortlisted for the John Bray National Poetry Award. In 1987 she was one of the five poets representing Australia at the Struga International Poetry Festival. Her second book, *Fish-rings on Water*, was published by Forest Books, London and introduced by Peter Porter. In 1994, her translation from French of Jean-Jacques Celly's poems, *The Sleepwalker with Eyes of Clay*, introduced by Peter Florence, was published by Forest Books. In 2000, her third full collection, *Tigers on the Silk Road* was published by Arc Publications and she was awarded a Royal Literary Fund Award. In 2005, Vagabond Books, Sydney, published her chapbook, *After Kandinsky*, in their 'Rare Object Series'. In 2006, Arc Publications published her fourth collection *Circus-Apprentice*, and in 2010, *Carnival Edge: New & Selected Poems*.

From 2002-8, she was Education Officer for Writers Inc and from July-October, 2002, Writer in Residence at Railway Fields Nature Reserve, Harringay, London. In 2008, she received a London Society of Authors' Foundation Award. Her poems were featured on the A.B.C's POETICA programme, Radio National, in June, 2009; the programme was repeated two years later. In 2012, she represented Australia as a Parnassus Poet at the Derry Tall Ships' Homecoming Celebrations, Northern Ireland. .

In November, 2012, Carol Rumens chose her poem 'The Year of the Tree' for the *Guardian* blog's Poem of the Week, and in 2015, Andrew Spicer made it into a film, featuring Molly Byrne and presented on Vimeo.

She has read her poetry at festivals and universities in the UK, Australia, Ireland, Germany, Italy and France and her poems have been translated into French, German, Hebrew, Italian, Romanian and Serbo-Croat.

www.katherine-gallagher.com

ACKNOWLEDGEMENTS

'Credo' appeared in The Best Australian Poems 2012 (ed. John Tranter, Black Inc) and 'The Mastery of Horses' in The Best Australian Poems 2014, (ed. Geoff Page, Black Inc); 'Bees' was included in The Price of Gold (Grey Hen Press, 2012; 'Birthday Owl' was published in Fanfare (Second Light Publications, 2015) and 'Quotidian' in Wheel of the Stars, (Ver Poets' Fiftieth Anniversary Anthology, 2016).

A group of the author's haiku were published in The First Australian Haiku Anthology (Paper Wasp, 2003), The Iron Book of British Haiku (Iron Press, 1998) and still heading out (an anthology of Australian and New Zealand haiku, Paper Wasp, 2013).

'Finding the Prince', 'Coming into Zurich', 'Lonesome Tonight' and 'Chartres' (published here as 'A Measure of Stillness' first appeared in the pamphlet Finding the Prince (Hearing Eye, 1993). 'Bullies' was published in Them and Us (Bodley Head, 1993).

Acknowledgement is due to Jean Boase-Beier for use of her translation 'Mother Tongue' by Rose Ausländer as an epigraph.

Acknowledgements are also due to the editors of the following magazines and newspapers: (in the UK) Acumen, ARTEMIS Poetry, Blithe Spirit, Daily Express, Poetry Review, The French Literary Review, Ware Poets Anthology, and the online magazine London Grip; (in Australia) The Age, The Australian Book Review, Quadrant, Weekend Review and the online magazines Communion, Foame; (in India) Prosopisia.

CPSIA information can be obtained
at www.ICGtesting.com
Printed in the USA
BVOW03s0843150817
492102BV00001B/24/P